D1014850

a cynic's guide to
a rich and full life

by
Mario DiGiorgio

Published by Last Gasp of San Francisco
777 Florida Street, San Francisco, California, 94110
www.lastgasp.com

Printed in China by Prolong Press Ltd.

10 9 8 7 6 5 4 3 2

ISBN-10: 0-86719-755-2
ISBN-13: 978-0-86719-755-6

Please note that if you are offended by any of the following
content, the author strongly suggests you educate yourself on
the finer points of parody. Getting offended is just insecurity
with a fake nose and mustache. Evolve.

Cover design by Mario DiGiorgio
Photos by Sheila Talbitzer and Mario DiGiorgio
Inspired by H. Jackson Brown, Jr.

Don't forget to visit www.mariosomething.com

INTRODUCTION

Kudos to you, my dear consumer, for you have just made the wisest purchase since Jefferson plunked down three cents an acre for one quarter of this great, great country of ours. That is, assuming you paid for it.

People say that what you give is what you get. That you need to slow down and soak in life. Stop and smell the bacon. People will also tell you that the essence of joy is found within the appreciation of the little things. Simply put, those people are idiots.

Planting a garden will leave you with sore knees and throbbing blisters. Taking the scenic route will make you tardy. Furthermore, you cannot pay your mortgage with the laughter of children.

Someone reminded me of life's three R's: Responsibility for one's actions; Respect for one's self; Respect for others. Here's one more: Really? When is the last time you witnessed anyone living by these logical, yet seemingly unattainable standards?

People are still dinging my car and driving off. Still using religion as a green light for hate. And I'm still waiting for a restaurant with a no-kids section.

Some folks insist on seeking out the good in people. But you know better. You know there comes a time when children need tripping, dolphins need flogging, and by gum, old people need a-murderin'.

Not surprisingly, the bulk of society frowns on that sort of behavior. So I offer you this black cloud of unconventional wisdom to quell those dark urges; a collection of joyfully inappropriate wishful thinking that would dampen the days of those near and not so dear. Anyone can hold a door open for a stranger. However, it takes a rare and special breed to trip them in the process. Sigh. If only.

So I urge you, hesitant reader, plant your tongue firmly in cheek and prepare to learn the secrets of living a truly rich and full life.

-MD

Dream the dream some men only dream of,
and let your inspiration inspire you.

Compliment three people every day.
Insult four.

♦

Instead of driving to work today,
quit your job.

♦

Take a kid to the zoo.
Then leave him there.

Every year, send out at least a dozen
Christmas cards. All addressed to your
Jewish neighbor.

◆

Help a child plant a garden.
They have no idea what
pot looks like.

◆

Overtip a breakfast waitress.
Then walk the check.

Learn to recognize the insignificant.
Then ignore it. Then divorce it.

♦

Don't outlive your money.
Spend that last $11.50
and *then* jump.

♦

Street musicians are a treasure.
Make a small donation, then tell
them they suck.

Dance like nobody's watching.
Then apologize to those who were.

♦

Be a good loser.
Practice makes perfect. Loser.

♦

Have impeccable manners.
Learn to belch the phrase: "Pardon me."

Greet the mailman.
With a pitbull.

♦

If you get really angry, stick your hands in
your pockets. And diddle yourself.

♦

Give someone a back rub,
then feel them up.

Ask your grandparents to tell you a
story about their childhood.
On your marks. Get set. Yawn!

♦

Help someone find a lost pet.
Show them where you buried it.

♦

Watch what you ingest at cocktail parties.
That goes double at orgies.

Give confidence to others.
Gain fifty pounds.

♦

If you like someone, let them know.
Sometimes you only have one chance
to get rejected.

♦

Be your spouse's best friend.
Then *do* your spouse's best friend.

When reading self-help books,
include the Bible.
Then ignore and distort His message
like a good Christian.

Always order bread pudding
if it's on the menu.
Just what you need. More bread.

♦

Take advantage of a loved one.

♦

Believe in love at first glance.
But don't hold your breath,
you hideous fuck.

Make someone's day by not speaking.

♦

If something seems too good to be true,
it probably is.
Check for an Adam's apple.

♦

Wash your whites separately. Racist.

Redeem gift certificates promptly. Those "massage clinics" don't stay in business for long.

◆

Stay in shape. Pear-shape.

◆

Never refuse a homemade brownie. From Tommy Chong.

Take the time to laugh at
someone's disability.

♦

Always leave the toilet seat in the
down position. While you pee.

♦

Learn to juggle. Kittens.

Every now and again
let your spirit of adventure
triumph over your good sense.
What I'm saying is,
let's do the intercourse.

Associate with people smarter than you.
For example: everyone else.

♦

Show respect to living things.
Your crabs have feelings, too.

♦

Never underestimate the power of
forgiveness. That reminds me,
I fucked your best friend.

Buy your fiance the most elegant
engagement ring you can afford.
After all, she's giving you a lifetime
of compromise.

◆

Respect tradition. Leave the money on
the dresser on your way out.

◆

Accept your limitations.
Stop trying to suck your own dick.

Purchase a fresh box
of 64 crayons.
Lie on the floor and
see how many you can
fit in your butthole.

Be big enough to admit your mistakes.
Then take them all out
for happy meals.

♦

Drink champagne for no reason at all,
every day for six months.

♦

Praise in public, but criticize in private.
Wait, reverse that.

Sign and carry your organ donor card.
Directly above your signature, write:
"BALLS ONLY."

♦

Say "thank you" a lot. During sex.

♦

Leave everyone laughing.
Then again, just leave.

Rub a dog's belly. De-claw a cat.

♦

Wear audacious underwear
under the most solemn business attire.
Whore.

♦

Pursue old-fashioned games
and activities. Like Scrabble, or
dry humping.

Go to where you can hear a wooden screen door slam shut. Then tell those hicks to fix their fucking door.

♦

Wear polished shoes. At the gym.

♦

Meet with people who hold vastly different views than you. Someone sane would be nice.

Carry a small Swiss Army knife
on your keychain.
And a tiny Cub Scout in your purse.

◆

Don't take 12 items to the
10 items or less lane.
Take 30. And a .45.

◆

Always accept a helping hand. It's not
every day you get a reacharound.

When you're a passenger in someone's car, never complain about the music. Just stop carpooling with Mexicans.

Memorize your favorite love poem.
Then recite it to your 37 cats.

♦

Take off your sunglasses when you
talk to someone. But keep them on
when you fuck someone.

♦

Think twice before
accepting the lowest bid.
Your virginity is priceless.

When taking a woman home, make sure
she's safely inside her house
before you park and masturbate.

♦

Attend a local chili cook-off.
Then take a bath with a loved one.

♦

Attend a high school
gymnastics meet. Lick your lips
repeatedly.

Spend the afternoon in an art gallery.
Don't forget your magic markers.

♦

Never call a rifle a "gun," a ship a
"boat," or my big fat cock a "penis."

♦

Every age brings new opportunities.
And you're never too old
to ignore them.

This father's day, call your dad.
An asshole.

♦

There are people who will always come
up with reasons why you can't do
what you want to do.
Listen to those people.

♦

Liven up your regular diet with
ethnic cuisines. Blow a Cuban.

Give disadvantaged children a reason
to laugh. Show them an even *more*
disadvantaged child.

♦

Send a love-letter. To a bum.

♦

Spice things up in the bedroom:
hire a hooker.
Condoms? Not tonight.

Ignorance may be bliss,
but it's also expensive.
You poor, happy idiot.

Take a kid to visit the local fire
station. At random, point out
which firefighters are gay.

♦

Never get a tattoo. On your taint.
Or *of* your taint.

♦

Own a comfortable chair for reading.
Then fuck in it.

Memorize the state capitals.
You'll be the smartest employee
at Wendy's.

♦

Pray for an enemy. To die.

♦

Win without boasting. Better yet,
boast without winning.
It's the American way!

Give your spouse handmade
"love coupons." Expiration date:
yesterday.

♦

Don't be afraid to say:
"I don't know" or "I made a mistake."
Actually, go ahead and get used to it.

♦

Don't let people see you tipsy.
Especially your sponsor.

If you're in a fight,
hit first and hit hard. And be quick...
your kids'll be home soon.

♦

Let teenagers know that they
are loved. White lies are good
for your soul.

♦

Keep good company. Nice people can
always use a scapegoat.

Be more romantic in the bedroom.
Chuck a towel over the wet spot.

♦

Don't be critical of your wife's friends.
Just smile and ignore the stoopit bitches.

♦

Always fasten the strap around your neck
before looking through binoculars.
And turn off your bedroom light.

Once a year, go someplace
you've never been to.
Like Europe. Or the dentist.

♦

Offer a beverage to a plumber or
cable installer. Then pour it down
their ass-crack.

♦

Don't shy away from going on blind dates.
After all, it's how I met my mistress.

When you're angry with someone,
write a letter telling them why.
But don't mail it.
Use it to give them a paper cut.

♦

Never cheat.
Scratch that. Never get caught.

♦

Buy your kids educational toys.
Like a metric scale and tiny baggies.

Feeling homesick?
Take a trip with your mother.
To the OBGYN.

♦

When passing a wishing well,
toss in a coin.
And the murder weapon.

♦

Become the kind of person who lights up
a room, just by leaving it.

Silence is sometimes the best answer.
Especially if the question is,
"Do you take this man..."

♦

Keep your promises. Pull out this time.

♦

Get professional advice from
professionals. Your friends have
no idea how to deep throat.

Make it a habit to do
nice things for people
who will never find out.
Then again,
fuck that shit.

Let bad news in the left
ear and out the right.
Yup. That'll cure the cancer.

♦

Don't flush urinals with your hand.
Use your cock.

♦

Commit yourself to constant improvement.
Step one: stop talking.

When tempted to criticize your
parents, spouse or children,
take a deep breath, count to ten
and go for it.

♦

Accept pain and disappointment
as part of life.
You didn't *have* to get married.

To battle the blues, try exercising.
Still down? Try cutting yourself.

♦

Almost everything looks better after a
good night's sleep. Except him.

♦

Always stand when
greeting a visitor into your office.
Or your orifice.

Don't ever mention being on a diet.
Who's going to believe your fat ass?

♦

Keep your private thoughts private.
Except thoughts about your privates.

♦

Be the first to welcome the
new kid at school.
With a series of purple nurples.

Pet puppies at the local animal
shelter. *Of Mice and Men* style, yo.

◆

Feed the soul. Gummy Bears and blow.

◆

Celebrate animal kindness week.
Teabag a dachshund.

Remember the three
universal healers:
Chicken soup,
calamine lotion and
cunnilingus.

Attend class reunions.
Make fun of the losers, all over again.

♦

Learn how to slow dance.
With a deer carcass.

♦

To explain a break-up, simply say:
"It was all my fault, I don't
get along with assholes."

Tape record your mother's laughter. Play it at your father's funeral.

♦

Be cautious about lending money to friends, as you might lose them. Lend it to family. Same reason.

Learn to paddle a canoe.
Then learn to fuck in one.

♦

Fly a kite with a child.
Higher! Higher! Now cut the string.

♦

When asked to play the piano,
do it without complaining.
But use your elbows.

Don't pray for things,
pray for wisdom
and courage...the courage to
steal those things.

When there's no time for a
full workout, fuck a personal trainer.

♦

Give five percent of your income
to charity. Sure, that's just her stage
name, but she earns every penny.

♦

Frame anything your kid brings home
from school. Like a painting,
or head lice.

Every little thing you do matters.
April fools.

◆

Instead of using the words, "If only,"
replace them with, "Who am I kidding?"

◆

Never approach horses or restaurants
from the rear. Especially restaurants
that serve horse.

Remember, there is immeasurable power in prayer. When I say, "immeasurable," I mean, "fictitious."

♦

Whistle. In church.

♦

Light candles and listen to Mozart. Don't own any Mozart? Good for you.

When travelling on back roads, stop when you see a sign that reads, "Honey for sale." Then inquire, "Well, where *is* the bitch?"

Don't postpone joy.
Jerk off right away.

♦

Drop off a pizza at the local
police station. Top it with
pepperoni and loose gravel.

♦

Use the photo of a loved one as
a bookmark. In a Hustler.

Remember that overnight success takes about ten years. Nobody starts out as head sandwich artist.

♦

Never speed or drive recklessly with kids in the car.
Well, not with *your* kids.

♦

Tour your state capitol building.
In a Speedo.

Never mind the Joneses,
keep up with the Jews.

♦

Applaud the piano player at a bar.
Slow, sarcastic applause.

♦

Watch your back, your weight and your
language. You paranoid, chubby fuck.

Never accept a job that requires you
to work in an office with no windows.
Or a glory hole.

.♦

Visit a pet store and watch the children
watching the animals. Perv.

♦

Feed a stranger's parking meter,
then slash the tires.

Every once in a while,
trip a child.

♦

Never call anyone stupid,
even if you're kidding.
And I'm not even kidding. Stupid.

♦

Bake a batch of sweet-smelling
gingerbread cookies, then chuck
them at old people.

Never tell a man
he's losing his hair.
Just point and laugh.

Stop taking things so
personally. You stupid fuck.

♦

Learn to identify local
wildflowers, trees and birds.
Then prepare for a life of
crushing loneliness.

♦

Don't ignore hunches.
He's probably cheating on you.

Be the first to end an argument
with your mother.
Besides, nothing beats make-up sex.

♦

Pin up photos of exotic places
in your cubicle. It will help
delay suicide.

♦

Don't let your possessions possess your
precious time. Hire a nanny.

Always put something in the
collection plate. Like shirt buttons
or broken glass.

♦

Lend a hand.
Then yank it away real quick.

♦

Learn three squeaky-clean jokes.
Then go wash your vagina, you wuss.

Never say,
"My child would never do that..."
to another parent.
Unless your next sentence is:
"...because he's dead."

♦

Don't go to bed with
dirty dishes in the sink. Put them
in your roommate's closet.

Well-behaved women
rarely make history.
They make breakfast.

Wear a tie with a cartoon character
on it if you work with kids. Or idiots.

♦

Always show respect to your elders.
Your elders with money.

♦

Send an anonymous gift of money
to your favorite charity.
Don't forget to cancel the check.

Be loving to people who don't love you.
After all, they're your parents.

♦

Tell someone how great they look.
Try to keep a straight face.

♦

When boarding a bus, say
"Hello" to the driver. When
getting off, remember to
mutter, "Loser."

Surprise an old friend
with a phone call.
Then hang up on them.

♦

It's a beautiful day.
Steal a car with a sunroof.

♦

Skip the rice cakes this
morning, eat a bag a flour.

Nibble a piece of chocolate to cure bad
breath from garlic or onions,
or cock.

♦

Find a local carnival and ride
the ferris wheel.
Then blow a carnie.

♦

Invite the person in line behind
you to go ahead of you.
Gently caress their inner thigh.

Never make fun of people who
speak broken English.
It means they know
another language.
And they will cut you.

Watch old episodes of
"The Andy Griffith Show."
Sucks, doesn't it?

♦

Sing in a choir. Off key.
Then explain, "It's because
Jesus hates me."

Never ask anyone why they wear
a Medic Alert bracelet. Just yank it off
and play "keep-away."

♦

Stop apologizing. It's getting annoying.

♦

Don't spend time worrying
who's right. It's probably not you.

Never tell anyone they don't have a
good sense of humor.
Just stop hanging out with
conservatives.

♦

Throw a surprise party for a good
friend. Then tell him the day after.

♦

Do not cause another to suffer,
break off the engagement today.

Keep your desk or work area
neat and tidy. What I'm saying is,
clear that shit off your dashboard.

♦

Let people pull in front of you
in traffic. Wave them in with
your middle finger.

Teach someone how to use
a thesaurus.
Begin with the word "ignorant."

♦

Smile and wave at crosswalk patrol
moms. Then toss 'em your motel key.

♦

Revive a long-lost art form.
Hand-jobs, for example.

Put a condiment smiley face on a kid's sandwich. When he takes a bite, shriek: "Murderer! You've killed Captain Smiles!"

Don't undertip the waiter if the food is bad; he didn't cook it. However, there's a good chance he came in it.

♦

Build a tree house for a child.
Out of balsa wood.

♦

Greet your grandmother with a kiss.
Open mouth with a splash of tongue.

Let go of unrealistic expectations.
She is never going to fuck you.

♦

When you hear a kind word
about a friend, tell him so.
But tell him it sounded sarcastic.

♦

Whenever you take something back for a
refund or exchange, wear a coat and tie.
You'll be the best-dressed guy
at Dildo Hut.

Don't compare your children with their friends or siblings. Trust me. Worst. Buyer's remorse. Ever.

♦

What you must do, do regretfully.

♦

Offer to polish the toenails of a pregnant woman. Using a Sharpie, write "Ozzy Rulez" across her toes.

Always return shopping carts
to the same place you found them.
Upside down at the bus stop.

♦

When you see a lady standing, be a
gentleman and offer her your lap.

♦

Take your best friend to an
expensive lunch. After dessert,
tell them you forgot your wallet.

Don't let a few dollars keep you from getting what you really want. Besides, the Asian ones let you pee on them.

Why not take the scenic route home?
That's an extra ten minutes you won't
have to spend with *him*.

◆

Enjoy homemade s'mores.
Wash them down with Wild Turkey.

◆

Learn to play "Me So Horny"
on the piano.

Ride a bike. Through the hallway
of an amputee ward.

♦

Hug a cow. Rape an ostrich.

♦

Be sure to stop and look up when
anyone approaches your desk.
Then stare at their crotch.

Pay for a poor child to go to summer camp. The rich kids need someone to pick on.

♦

Don't forget safety glasses when
operating a power saw.
You don't wanna get blood in your eyes.

♦

Start a donation box for a local charity.
When it's full, treat yourself to a
steak dinner.

Send your aging
grandmother
a large arrangement of
flowers for no reason.
Attach a card that reads,
"Any day now."

Listen to the whole answer.
Then mock accordingly.

♦

Direct your own future.
But cast someone better looking
to play you.

♦

Learn a new language.
Just the curse words.

Offer to run an errand for your
spouse, then fall asleep on the couch.

♦

Remember that cruel words
can deeply hurt. That's good
information to have.

♦

Also remember that loving words
can quickly heal.
So keep those to yourself.

Learn the Heimlich maneuver.
Use it when someone
tries to hug you.

♦

Enter a contest...you might win!
But probably not.

♦

Do not jump to conclusions.
Maybe the FedEx guy really *was*
giving your husband a rectal exam.

Here comes Santa Claus. Here comes Santa Claus. Grab a towel.

◆

Keep a blanket
and a gallon of water in your trunk.
That hooker's gonna be chilly and
thirsty when she wakes up.

◆

You're dreaming of a white Christmas?
Well then, happy holidays. Racist.

Ladies, kick things up
in the bedroom tonight.
Douche with Red Bull.

Wash your hands with lavender soap, treat yourself to a manicure and coat with peppermint lotion. That'll get the blood out.

♦

Donate books to a retirement home. Tear out the last 20 pages from each one.

♦

Say hello to people on the elevator, using your 'retardo' voice.

Celebrate this moment.
She'll be awake soon.

♦

Watch the movie, *Regarding Henry*.
You will laugh your ass off.

♦

Every now and again, bite off
more than you can chew.
Then hit the bathroom, bingey-purgey.

Attend the church of a small town.
Every now and again,
yell out, "Bullshit!"

♦

When passing a school bus, give
children the finger.

♦

Volunteer for a suicide hotline.
In a sultry voice, ask each caller
"So, what are you wearing, coward?"

Make yourself
a hot fudge sundae and
eat it in bed.
You fat piece of shit.

When a loved one becomes ill,
remember that hope is powerful
medicine. It's like penicillin, only useless.

♦

Visit a petting zoo;
a heavy petting zoo.

♦

Read the Wall Street Journal on the train.
Keep shouting, "Where the fuck is the
Jumble?!"

Put your jacket around your girlfriend
on a chilly night.
At least until the roofie kicks in.

♦

There's nothing like fresh-cut firewood.
From a child's treehouse.

♦

Sock away ten percent of what you earn.
At twenty bucks a hand job,
that starts to add up.

Contribute something to
each Salvation Army kettle
you pass during
the holidays.
Gum wrappers. Lint.
Loogey. Whatever.

Anything worth doing is going to take longer than you think.
And doing anyone worthwhile will be over before you know it.

◆

Go to an outdoor concert.
And masturbate.

◆

Make your money *before* spending it.
In this order: fucky, sucky, food, shoes.

Find a truly meaningful career.
In pornography.

♦

Play catch with a child.
That is, toss the kid to another adult.

♦

Visit your city's night court
on a Saturday evening.
Keep pulling your junk out
while shouting, "Withdrawn!"

When opportunity knocks,
hide behind the couch.
It'll go away eventually.

Don't ever buy a coffee table
you can't put your feet on.
Or do coke off of.

♦

If you dial a wrong number, apologize.
Then tell them you're not
wearing any pants.

♦

When disagreeing with your spouse,
don't bring up the past.
Wait, that's impossible, you're a woman.

Leave a dollar where a kid can find it.
On top of the stove or at the
bottom of a well.

◆

Share the credit, not the blame.

◆

Never leave clumps of hair in the drain,
toothpaste in the sink, or
DNA on the toilet seat.

Life will sometimes
hand you a magical
moment. Savor it.
Anal is hard to come by.

Watch a sunrise at least once a year.
You fucking drunk.

♦

See everything in your life as a gift.
A gift from a store that
went out of business.

♦

Write down three things that
were great about today.
I know, neither can I.

Thank the garbage collector
personally. Then toss an apple core
out the window of your Lexus.

◆

Spread a little joy. Then ask Joy
if she has a sister.

◆

Give a little heart to someone
who is down. No wait,
I mean head.

Get a facial at a beauty school.
Then give one.

♦

Feel an intimate connection with
the earth. Fuck a mud puddle.

♦

Take your dad to the movies.
But make him wait in the car.

Never miss an opportunity
to dance with your wife.
Those poles can support two people.

♦

Learn to say, "I have the diarrhea"
in French, Italian and Korean.

♦

Write and send letters to
representatives in Washington, D.C.
Begin each one, "Dear Douchebag."

Plant zucchini only if you
have a lot of friends.
A lot of lonely,
horny, female friends.

If you know you're about to lose,
do it with style. You should be
quite stylish by now.

♦

Spend the day bringing warmth and
happiness to those around you.
Do something vague and ambiguous
like the previous sentence.

♦

Love thy neighbor as thyself.
Fuck the restraining order.

Burn a CD of feel-good songs,
then give it to a homeless guy.

♦

Feed the ducks. Alka-Seltzer.

♦

Buy two copies of a book
so you can read it with your
sweetheart. Oh that's right,
you live alone.

When a stranger sneezes,
punch them in the neck.

♦

Ask a new parent to show you
pictures of their new baby.
Then recoil in disgust.

♦

Never lose your nerve or your temper.
Your virginity? Sure, go nuts.

Learn to forgive yourself.
Then get rid of the body.

♦

If you borrow a friend's car, return it
on time and fill it with gas.
Not fuel. Egg farts and methane.

♦

Call when you're running
ten minutes late. Then show up
in forty.

Shift the tone of an argument
with humor and jokes.
About their mother.

♦

Remember that winners do
what losers refuse to do...
brown nose, back stab and suck dick.

♦

Create a "bad day survival kit"
filled with things that give you
confidence, like tequila and meth.

Hire a maid service for the day. Spend the afternoon pointing at your crotch saying, "You missed a spot."

Resist giving advice about matrimony,
hairstyles or finances.
Unless you're divorced, bald and broke.

♦

Take a small gift to a dinner party.
Like a bucket of chicken, or
anal beads.

♦

Don't burden a friend with a secret.
No one needs to know about
your large ass fetish.

Sing in the shower.
Jerk off in a recording studio.

♦

Take your kid on a tour of a local
university. Point to the groundskeeper
and the parking lot attendant and say,
"Someday, son. Someday."

♦

Learn to fake enthusiasm.

If someone gives you something,
never say, "You shouldn't have."
Just maintain eye contact
while you drop kick it.

♦

Forgive someone quickly.
Plot revenge slowly.

♦

Encourage children to join a choir.
Little, gay children.

Cherish your kids for what they are.
Serves you right for smoking
through your pregnancy.

♦

Look for happiness in the least likely
places. Your marriage, for example.

♦

Go to the 'free night' at a local museum.
Keep mumbling under your breath,
"Well, you get what you pay for."

Carry a list of your wife's sizes
in your wallet. Then again, how hard
is it to remember "XXL?"

♦

Get to know your children's friends.
Bunch of weiners, aren't they?

♦

Remember, a kind word goes a long way.
But an insult goes even further.
It's like a kind-word javelin.

Never be ashamed of laughter
that's too loud, unless you're
around other people.

♦

When your child is sleeping, whisper into
his ear: "You were an accident."

♦

If you see someone sitting alone on a
bench, make it a point to speak to them.
In tongues.

Find someone who can
always be trusted.
Then find a unicorn that
farts rainbows.

Tape a positive message to the
bathroom mirror like,
"Lookin' good" or
"There's always suicide."

♦

Avoid sarcasm.
Right. That'll happen.

♦

Buy a world globe. It will provide
an idea of how many millions
of people don't give a shit about you.

Put a love note in your wife's luggage before she leaves on a trip.
And ladies, write a *Dear John* letter before you go.

♦

Clip your toenails in private.
But trim your privates in public.

♦

Never be ashamed of your patriotism.
Unless you live in another country, faggot.
USA! USA!

Spend your time creating,
not criticizing.
Unless you're a paid critic.
In that case, spend your time
eating a dick.

Take a little vacation from your
desk at lunchtime.
Hang out in the shitter.

◆

Leave a small gift or bouquet of
flowers on someone's desk
with a card that reads,
"Good Morning! You're Fired."

◆

Fly Old Glory on the fourth of
July, under a homemade pirate flag.

On a gloomy day, put sunny yellow napkins on the table. It'll brighten up your trailer.

♦

Watch your back. Your back fat.

♦

Change the usual way you have always done something. Use the opposite hand this morning.

Someone told me it's not my job
to get people to like me;
it's my job to like people. So I quit.

◆

Throw your towels in the dryer
right before you use them.
Ain't nothin' like a piping-hot cum rag.

◆

Don't drink anything blue.
And don't blow anything drunk.

The bible teaches us not to
covet thy neighbor's wife.
That is such bullshit,
hast thou seen that ass?

♦

Put a love note in your child's
lunchbox. In lieu of food.

♦

Volunteer to read at a retirement home.
Dressed as Death.

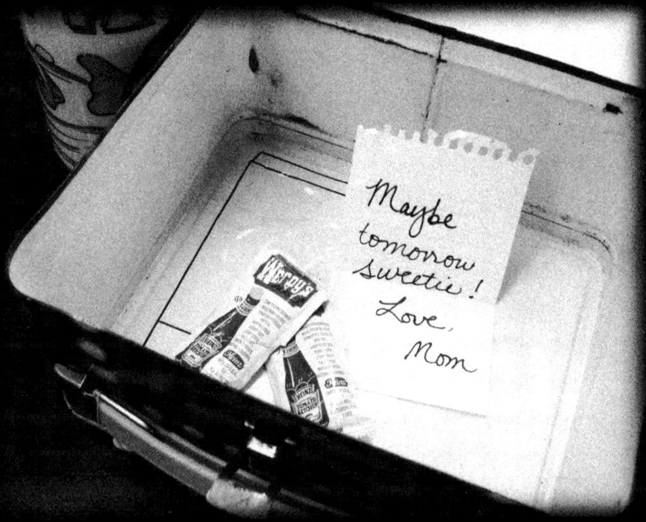
Maybe tomorrow sweetie!
Love,
Mom

This December, build a snowman with your kids. Don't forget the carrot nose and corncob cock.

♦

Keep your eyes on the prize. Chances are, you'll never actually touch it.

♦

Purchase a "Baby on Board" decal. Stick it on your luggage.

Never buy a cheap motorcycle helmet.
Unless it's a gift.

♦

When there's a piano to be moved,
reach for the stool while groaning,
"Little help?"

♦

Never say anything uncomplimentary
about someone's child. Unless they lisp.
Holy thit, that'h hilariouth.

Remember that life's most treasured moments often come unannounced.
But yes, I'm sorry
I came unannounced.

Take your son bowling.
Every time he hits the gutter,
tell him he's adopted.

♦

Never scoff at anyone's dreams.
Let them fail on their own.

♦

Hold the elevator door open
to let somebody on.
Then let one rip.

Volunteer to be a little league
umpire, then call nothing but strikes.

◆

Buy a few things from a high school
art show. Then start a bonfire.

◆

Never go to a grocery store when
you're hungry. And never, ever go
to a livestock show when you're horny.

Don't expect your love alone to change
a messy person into a neat one.
You have to beat them
with a vacuum hose.

♦

When shaking a woman's hand, don't
squeeze it harder than
she squeezes yours.
And don't let go for two minutes.

Never walk out on an argument
with your spouse...without saying,
"I'm sorry I married you."

♦

Stay clear of envy.
Concentrate on greed, sloth and lust.

♦

It is said that the more you know,
the less you fear.
You must be one frightened mofo.

Try to see things from other people's point of view. Perhaps you *are* a colossal bag of douche.

♦

Soak your hair in a hot-oil treatment. It'll wash out the semen.

♦

Visit a friend's new baby to cuddle and coo. Be sure to thank them for over-populating this fucking planet.

Don't ever admit at work that you're angry, tired, or bored. Just start yelling, yawning and yodeling.

♦

Stop to watch a farmer plowing.
His wife.

♦

Always introduce yourself to new neighbors. Tell them the law requires it.

When you answer the phone,
smile.
The caller will hear it in your voice.
Then take a wicked shit.
Hopefully, they'll hear that, too.

Learn a new card trick!
Then show it to your dog.
Seriously, no one else cares.

◆

Lie on your back and gaze at the stars.
It'll distract you from the fact that you're
fucking in a Best Buy parking lot.

◆

Take note of what's attractive about
other people. Like their absence.

Hug your children after
you discipline them.
Kids adore mixed messages.

♦

Seek out the good in people,
then exploit it.

♦

Take a brisk walk every morning.
Back to your sorority house.

Remember...the main thing is to keep the main thing the main thing.
And I got yer main thing right here.

Dress with respect
when attending church.
God only helps the fashionable.

♦

Buy a cowboy hat.
Wear it at the movies.

♦

Start a standing ovation at a
grade-school play. Stand and boo.

Usually jog three miles a day?
This morning, do it in a
wheel chair.

◆

When someone gives you exceptional
service, write a note to his or her pimp.

◆

Call in sick today.
You will not be missed.

Remember, one minute
of anger denies you sixty seconds
of happiness. Sweet.

◆

Obey all ten commandments. Nerd.

◆

Wake up and say aloud,
"I would like to make a difference today."
Then go back to sleep.

Laugh daily.
A good sense of humor
cures almost all of life's ills.
Unless you're poor.

"You're welcome."

Celebrated author
Mario DiGiorgio travels
the country spreading mirth
to the great unwashed; resides
in Austin and thinks you look
fat in those jeans.